Shark World

EXTREME
Sharks

ELLEN NORTHCUTT

SCHOLASTIC INC.

The publisher thanks the following for their kind permission to use their photographs in this book:

Photographs ©: cover: Dan Burton/Seapics.com; 1: Ethan Daniels/Shutterstock, Inc.; 3 center left center: Toui2001/Dreamstime; 3 top center: c-photo/iStockphoto; 3 top right: RainervonBrandis/iStockphoto; 3 bottom left: crisod/iStockphoto; 3 bottom right: cdascher/iStockphoto; 3 center left: DLILLC/Media Bakery; 3 center right: cesare naldi/Media Bakery; 3 top left: frantisekhojdysz/Shutterstock, Inc.; 3 center right center: Ethan Daniels/Shutterstock, Inc.; 4, 5: RapidEye/iStockphoto; 5 inset: skynesher/iStockphoto; 6 bottom inset: Sablin/iStockphoto; 6, 7: NaluPhoto/iStockphoto; 6 top inset: Ted Kinsman/Science Source; 8, 9 top: Masa Ushioda/Seapics.com; 9 bottom: bluehand/Shutterstock, Inc.; 10: Brandelet/Shutterstock, Inc.; 11: Comstock/Media Bakery; 12 right, 13: Marine Themes; 14: Norbert Wu/Science Faction/Superstock, Inc.; 15 inset: Gwen Lowe/Seapics.com; 15: Michael S. Nolan/Seapics.com; 16, 17 background: Brandelet/Shutterstock, Inc.; 17 top: Michele Westmorland/Media Bakery; 18: Makoto Hirose/Seapics.com; 19: David Shen/Seapics.com; 20: Stephen Frink/Media Bakery; 21: cdelacy/iStockphoto; 22: Doug Perrine/Seapics.com; 23: Tom McHugh/Science Source; 24, 25: NHPA/Superstock, Inc.; 26, 27: Beth Swanson/Shutterstock, Inc.; 28: Mark Conlin/Superstock, Inc.; 29 top: Georgette Douwma/Science Source; 29 bottom: Christian Musat/Shutterstock, Inc.; 30, 31: Stephen Frink Collection/Alamy Images; 32 Cookiecutter Shark: Roberto Nistri/Alamy Images; 32 Great White Shark: Willtu/Dreamstime; 32 Hammerhead: MR1805/iStockphoto; 32 Spotted Wobbegong Shark, 32 Dwarf Lantern Shark: Marine Themes; 32 Whale Shark: Comstock/Media Bakery; 32 Longnose Sawshark: Becca Saunders/Minden Pictures; 32 Basking Shark: Stefan Pircher/Shutterstock, Inc.; 32 Thresher Shark: Norbert Probst/imagebroker.net/Superstock, Inc.; 32 Short-Finned Mako Shark: Juniors/Superstock, Inc.; 32 Goblin Shark: Courtesy Dianne Bray/Museum Victoria, CC-BY.

ISBN 978-0-545-72501-9

12 11 10 9 8 7 6 5 4 3 2 1   14 15 16 17 18 19/0
Printed in the U.S.A.   40
First edition, September 2014

There are more than 350 kinds
of sharks. Some sharks are huge.
Others are tiny. And some look
quite strange!

Are you ready to learn about the
most extreme sharks?

Sharks are fish. Like other fish, sharks have gills. Gills let fish breathe underwater. Also, like other fish, sharks have fins that help them swim.

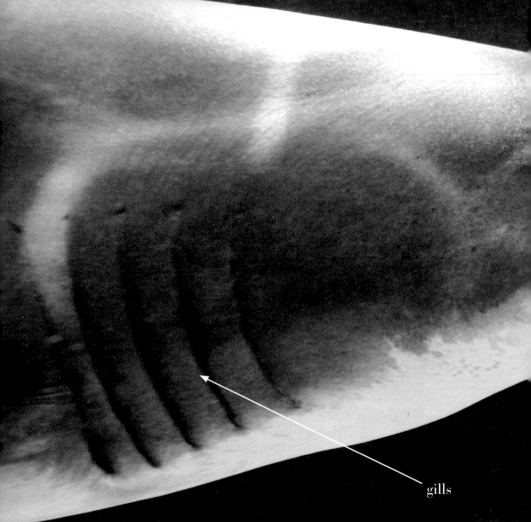

gills

But sharks are also different from other fish. Some fish can flap their fins. This lets them stop or swim backward. Sharks can't move their fins in this way.

flapping fins

There is another difference between sharks and other fish. Sharks have rough skin. Other fish have smooth scales.

Sharkskin is rough, like sandpaper.

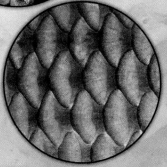

Fish scales are smooth and slippery.

Sharkskin is made of scales that are hard like teeth. The shape of the scales helps sharks move through the water.

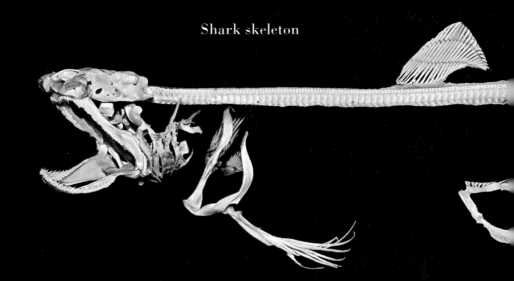

Shark skeleton

The biggest difference between sharks and other fish are bones. Sharks don't have hard bones. They have cartilage (CAR-till-edge). You can feel cartilage in your ears and the tip of your nose. It is stiff. But it also bends.

Other kinds of fish
have lots of bones.

Now that you know what
is special about sharks, let's
meet some different kinds.

The whale shark is the biggest fish in the ocean. It can grow bigger than a school bus.

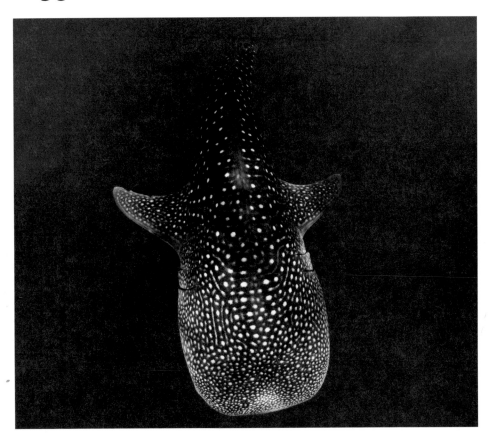

The stripes and spots on each whale shark are different.
No two whale sharks look exactly the same.

The whale shark keeps
its mouth open while it
swims slowly. Tiny animals
called plankton (PLANK-ton)
go into its giant mouth.
The shark swallows plankton
and other small fish. Then it
spits out the water.

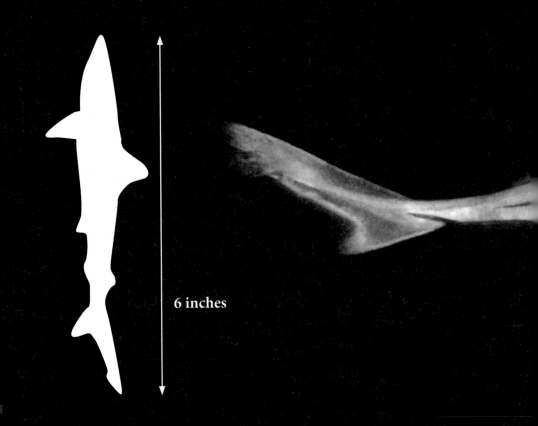

6 inches

The dwarf lantern is

the smallest shark! It is

only about six inches long.

But it eats the same food

as the huge whale shark.

Moller's Lantern Shark

There are different kinds of lantern sharks. They are called lantern sharks because they can light up! They live deep in the ocean, where it is very dark.

Cookiecutter sharks are less than two feet long. They don't use their sharp teeth to kill. They just take bites out of larger fish and even whales!

bite mark

Here is how a cookiecutter shark gets its name. It grabs on to an animal with its teeth and lips. Then it spins around. The bite mark makes a perfect circle.

Nothing else looks like
a hammerhead shark!
Its head is shaped
like a hammer!

Hammerheads have eyes on each end of their head. This helps hammerheads look for the animals they eat.

Hammerheads eat stingrays and other animals that hide in the sand. When they are really hungry, they sometimes eat other hammerheads.

The goblin shark lives in deep water. It has pink skin, small eyes, and a long, pointed nose, or snout. The goblin shark uses its snout to hunt and fight.

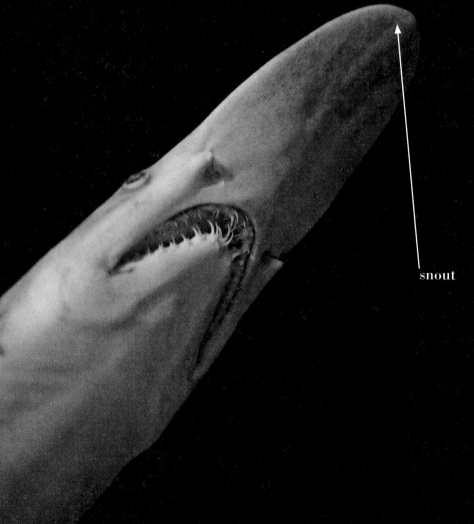

snout

A hungry goblin shark lifts its
snout to stick out its teeth. Then
it is ready to grab its food.

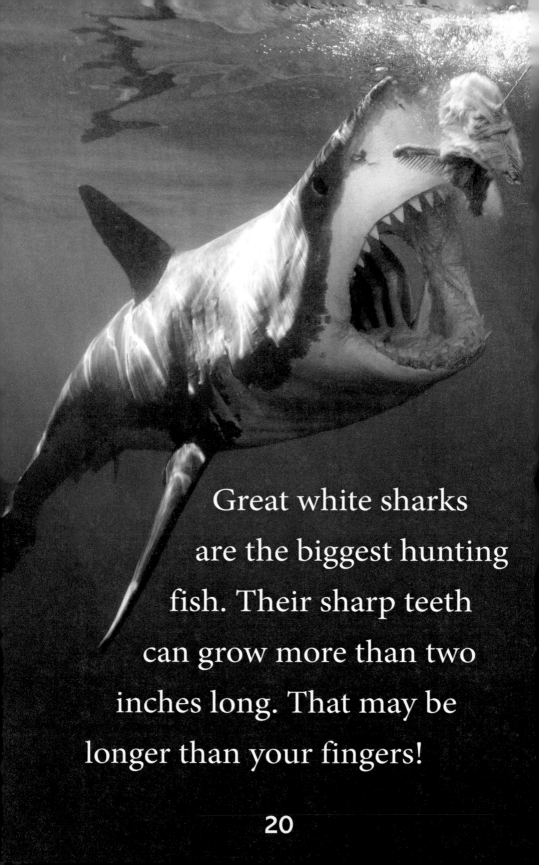

Great white sharks
are the biggest hunting
fish. Their sharp teeth
can grow more than two
inches long. That may be
longer than your fingers!

Great white sharks have super senses. They can smell a drop of blood in the water about a third of a mile away! That's about five football fields!

The spotted wobbegong
(WOE-bee-gong) is a flat
shark. It lives on the bottom
of the ocean. Some people call
it a carpet shark.

Can you see
this shark?

The spotted wobbegong waits for fish to swim by. Then it quickly opens its mouth and eats the fish.

Basking sharks can grow to more than thirty feet long. Some people think they look like sea monsters. But they are not dangerous to us.

Basking sharks are
like whale sharks.
They eat plankton
and tiny animals.

The bigeye (BIG-eye)
thresher shark has
the longest tail of all
sharks. Its tail can be
as long as its body.

The bigeye thresher shark swings its tail like a baseball bat. It hits smaller fish that swim by. Then the shark uses its tail to push the fish into its mouth.

Short-finned mako (MAY-ko) sharks are the fastest sharks. They can swim more than forty miles per hour. That's as fast as a car going down the street.

Short-finned mako
sharks can jump
up to twenty feet in
the air. That's high
enough to jump
over a giraffe!

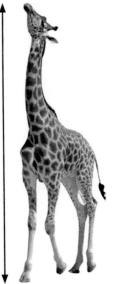

18 feet

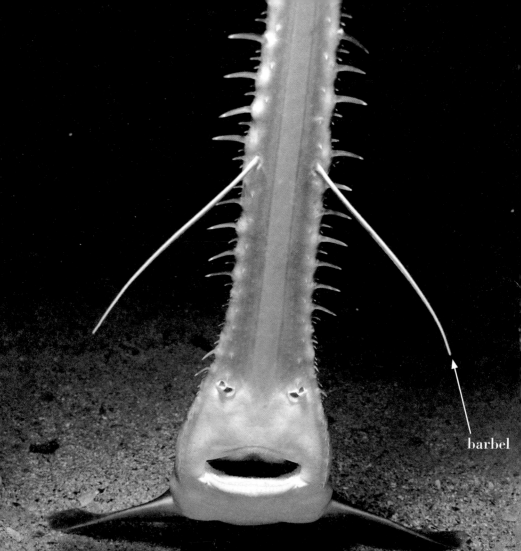

barbel

The longnose (LONG-nose) sawshark has a long, flat head and snout. The snout looks like a saw. It has large, sharp teeth on both sides.

This shark also has long whiskers called barbels. The shark uses its barbels to find animals that hide in the sand.

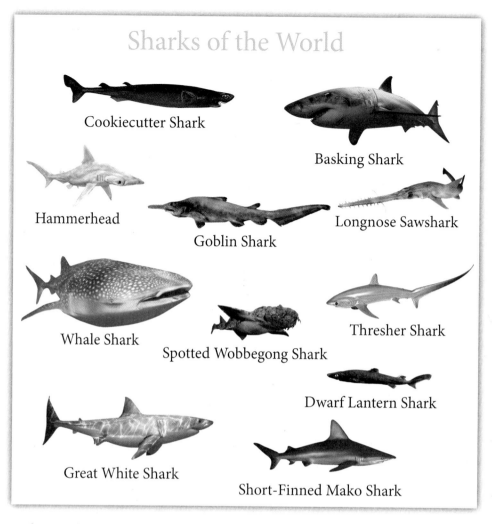

Cookiecutter Shark

Basking Shark

Hammerhead

Goblin Shark

Longnose Sawshark

Whale Shark

Spotted Wobbegong Shark

Thresher Shark

Dwarf Lantern Shark

Great White Shark

Short-Finned Mako Shark

Sharks live in every ocean of the world. They can be many different colors, shapes, and sizes. Which one do you think is the most extreme?